The Eager Witness

Raymond Chandler

GOGAKU SHUNJUSHA

*This book is published in Japan
by Gogaku Shunjusha Co., Inc.
2-9-10 Misaki-cho, Chiyoda-ku
Tokyo*

*First published 2006
© Gogaku Shunjusha Co., Inc.
Printed in Japan, All rights reserved.*

はしがき

　言語の学習にはテレビ，ビデオよりもラジオやCDのほうがはるかに適しているといわれる。それは音だけが唯一のコミュニケーションの手段だからだ。映像がない分，耳の働きは一層鋭敏になり，聴きとる力は確実にアップする。それは理論的にも証明済みである。
　アメリカで制作されたこの『イングリッシュ・トレジャリー（英語の宝箱）』は，その観点からリスニングの究極の教材といえるだろう。
　英米の名作，傑作が放送ドラマ形式で作られているので，登場人物のセリフがまるで目の前でしゃべっているかのように聞こえてくる。しかも，効果音が実によく挿入されているので，胸に迫る臨場感は格別だ。一瞬たりともリスナーの耳を離さないすばらしい出来栄えである。
　しかも，ドラマの出演者は，アメリカ・ハリウッド黄金時代を飾ったスターたちだ。人の言葉とはこんなに魅力あるものかと，あらためて感動を呼ぶ。
　『イングリッシュ・トレジャリー』のよさは，またその構成のうまさにあるといえよう。物語の進行に伴う場面ごとに適切なナレーションが入って，ストーリーの背景を説明してくれるので，リスナーの耳は瞬時にその場面に引き込まれる。そして，会話によどみがない。
　名作を十分堪能しながら，同時に総合的な語学学習ができるところに，この教材の利点がある。
　「リスニング力」の上達はもちろん，ストーリーの中で覚えられる「単語・会話表現」，そしてシャドウ（あとからついて言う）もでき，かつ，英語シナリオ一本まるごと読むことで身につく「読解力」と，まさに一石三鳥，いや四鳥の「英語の宝箱」だ。
　どの作品を取り上げても文句なく楽しめるシリーズだ。

CONTENTS

はしがき……………………………………………… iii
シリーズの使用法…………………………………… v
CD INDEX 一覧……………………………………… vi
解　説………………………………………………… vii
ものがたり…………………………………………… ix
SCENE 1 …………………………………………… 2
SCENE 2 …………………………………………… 14
SCENE 3 …………………………………………… 22
SCENE 4 …………………………………………… 32
SCENE 5 …………………………………………… 38
SCENE 6 …………………………………………… 52
SCENE 7 …………………………………………… 60
SCENE 8 …………………………………………… 68

●シリーズの使用法

英検1級レベル

　まず，英文シナリオを見ずにCDに耳を集中する。第2ステージでは，聞き取れなかった部分及び「これは」と思った慣用表現を英文シナリオでチェック。最終的には口頭でシャドウできるまで習熟することが目標です。

英検2級〜準1級レベル

　英文シナリオを参照しながら，CDを聴くことから始める。第2ステージでは，英文シナリオの完全理解を図る。と同時に，重要な会話表現や単語をどんどん身につけていく。第3ステージでは，対訳を参照しながら，CDを聴いてみよう。シナリオなしにCDが聞き取れるようになれば卒業だ。

英検3級〜準2級レベル

　対訳を参照しながら，まず英文シナリオをしっかり読む。第2ステージでは，英文シナリオを参照しながらCDを聴こう。音声のスピードに慣れるまでは，章ごとに切って，何度も聴きながら，学習を進めてください。未知の単語や会話表現をどんどん覚えるチャンスです。

　第3ステージでは，対訳を参照しながら，CDに集中する。この頃には，耳も相当慣れてきて，リスニングにかなりの手応えが感じられてくるだろう。

　物語の選択にあたっては，難易度表の「初級〜中級レベル」表示の比較的易しめのものから入っていくことをお勧めする。

CD INDEX 一覧

	本文ページ	該当箇所	冒頭部分
1	2	**SCENE 1**	Get this, and get it straight:...
2	14	**SCENE 2**	Another scotch and soda, mister?
3	22	**SCENE 3**	It was eight o'clock, and almost dark...
4	32	**SCENE 4**	As Mallory oozed towards the door I slid...
5	38	**SCENE 5**	It was strictly hit and run. I piled...
6	52	**SCENE 6**	For the second time that night I started...
7	60	**SCENE 7**	With Sharpe at the wheel of the pick-up truck,...
8	68	**SCENE 8**	Well, Gail, the big show's about to start.

（本CDは歴史的に貴重なオリジナル音源を使用しておりますので，一部お聴きぐるしい箇所が含まれている場合もございますが，ご了承ください）

解 説

　探偵フィリップ・マーロウを生み出したのは，シカゴ生まれ，英国育ちの作家，レイモンド・チャンドラー（Raymond Chandler：1888-1959）。

　離婚した母に連れられて英国に渡り，ロンドン郊外に住みはじめたのは，7歳のときだった。大学を中退してパリ，ミュンヘンに留学後，海軍省に勤めたものの半年で退職。新聞・雑誌に記事やエッセイを書いて生計を立てていたが，生活苦から，1912年，アメリカに戻る。

　簿記係などを経て，石油会社役員を務めていた44歳の時，不祥事や内輪揉めなどが原因で解雇された彼は，失意の渦中で作家になることを決意。処女短編「脅迫者は射たない」（Blackmailers don't Shoot：1933）を5か月かけて執筆し，パルプ・マガジン「ブラック・マスク」誌に発表した。

　1934年，チャンドラーは18歳年上のピアニスト，パール・ユージェニー・ハールバート（通称シシー）と結婚している。しかし，1954年に愛妻が死去した後は，過度の飲酒で度々体調を崩し，入退院を繰り返した。

　1959年，執筆中の『プードル・スプリングス物語』未完のまま急逝。

　チャンドラーは，ダシール・ハメット，ロス・マクドナルドとともに"アメリカのハードボイルド御三家"と称される。文学性が高く，ほとんど感傷的ともいえる独特の文体が持ち味で，推理よりはムードと人物像を描くことの名手として名高い。「チャンドラリアン」と呼ばれる熱狂的なファンに支持され，現在でも多くの読者に

愛されつづけている。

マーロウものはしばしばテレビ化・映画化もされた。

演じたのは，名優ハンフリー・ボガート，ロバート・モンゴメリー，エリオット・グールド，ロバート・ミッチャムら。

マーロウを主人公とする主な作品には，以下のようなものがある。

『大いなる眠り』（The Big Sleep：1939）

『さらば愛しき女よ』（Farewell, My Lovely：1940）

『高い窓』（The High Window：1942）

『湖中の女』（The Woman in the Lake：1943）

『かわいい女』（The Little Sister：1949）

『長いお別れ』（The Long Goodbye：1954）

『プレイバック』（Playback：1958）

ものがたり

　　ロサンゼルスで個人事務所を開業する私立探偵，フィリップ・マーロウのもとに，1件の依頼が舞い込んだ。競馬調教師カート・ハーパーのサンフランシスコ行きに同行し，身辺の警護にあたってほしいというものだ。しかし，仕事を引き受けたその日のうちに，依頼者ハーパーは殺害されてしまう。
　　容疑者はアール・ジャーニギン。逮捕はされても有罪になったことのない小狡(こず)い男で，今回の裁判でも，彼の弁護士は余裕の表情だ。
　　検察側証人として証言台に立ったマーロウが決定的な証言をした後でも，「反対尋問は必要ない」と言い放つ弁護側。
　　これは何かとんでもない隠しだまがあるにちがいない！
　　皆が固唾(かたず)をのんで見守るなか，ジャーニギンの証人として登場したのは，なんと地元の名士であり大不動産業者の，レナード・ゲインズその人だった。
　　父の敵討(かたきう)ちを心に誓うハーパーの娘ゲイルは，時間稼ぎに騒動を起こして裁判を中断させ，マーロウに調査協力を依頼する。
　　「レナード・ゲインズは嘘つきよ。ジャーニギンが父を殺した犯人だって証明したいの」
　　事件の鍵となるのは1通の手紙――マーロウは真相を探るため，ゲインズの前妻が滞在する温泉保養地へと向かうが，そこではまた新たな殺人事件が発生する……。

Marlowe:
(Narration)

Get this, and get it straight: crime is a sucker's road and those who travel it wind up in the gutter, the prison, or the grave. It started with a man on trial for his life, and an A-one citizen eager to testify. But there it was interrupted, and it wasn't until I found a corpse in a bubbling bath, gun play in the woods, and lots of blackmail that the real eager witness had a chance to talk.

1

Court Official:

(*hum of voices; sound of gaveling*)

Hear me, hear me. In the aid of the Superior Court of the State of California before the Country of Los Angeles now in session, the Honorable Albert Wisden, Judge, presiding, everybody rise.

Mar (Nar):

It was the case of the people versus the oft-arrested, never convicted, smooth Earl Jurnigen, sometimes bookie, charged in the first degree with the monthold killing of the kindly,

マーロウ(語り)： 　誤解のないように聞いておくんだな，犯罪とは愚か者の選ぶ道なんだ。その道を歩くやつは，結局貧乏暮らしか刑務所か，墓場の中に行きつくことになるものだ……。今度の事件の始まりは，ある男が死刑を宣告されるかもしれない罪で裁判にかけられ，町の名士である一市民が証言を買って出るという形だった。ところがこの証言は中断され，本当に熱意ある証人にようやく発言の機会がまわっていくまでには，まず，おれが温泉の中で死体を発見し，森の中でピストルを射ちあい，いくつもの恐喝事件に気づくことになったのだった。

(1)

（話し声。裁判長の槌の音）

裁判所の係官： 　全員静粛に。ただ今から，カリフォルニア州高等裁判所ロサンゼルス郡法廷は，アルバート・ウィスデン氏を裁判長として開廷いたします。一同起立。

マーロウ(語り)： 　事件の被告は，時にノミ屋を開業するアール・ジャーニギン，逮捕歴は多いが有罪になったことのない狡い男。今回，彼には，親切者で白髪頭の競馬調教師カート・ハーパーの第一級謀殺という，1か月前の事件の嫌疑がかかっている。こ

grey-haired horse-trainer named Kurt Harper, who had once almost been my client. It was the afternoon of the fourth day of the trial. The prosecutor for the state had already built almost air-tight case against the alleged gambler, when my turn finally came.

Prosecution: ....To further substantiate the state's claim that Earl Jurnigen did wilfully, with malice aforethought, take the life of the deceased Kurt Harper,...will Mr. Philip Marlowe take the stand?

CO: Raise your right hand. (*rapidly*) Do you vow to tell the truth, the whole truth, and nothing but the truth, so help you God?

Mar: I do.

Judge: State your name and occupation.

Mar: Philip Marlowe, private detective.

Judge: Take the stand. (*footsteps*)

Pros: Mr. Marlowe, on the morning of the 30th day of July last, the day on which the late Kurt Harper was murdered, were

のカート・ハーパーに，おれはもう少しで探偵として雇われるところだったのだ。裁判が始まって4日目の午後のことだった。検察官は，この賭博師(とばくし)といわれるアール・ジャーニギンに不利な証拠を，水ももらさぬほど完璧に積み重ねてきていたのだ。ここでようやくおれの出番が来た。

検察官： 被告アール・ジャーニギンが，故意にかつ予謀の殺意をもって故人カート・ハーパーを殺害したという，本官の主張を，さらに立証したいと存じます。フィリップ・マーロウさん，証人台にお立ちください。

係官： 右手を挙げて。（早口で）神に誓ってただ真実のみを述べると誓いますか。

マーロウ： 誓います。
裁判長： 姓名・職業を述べてください。
マーロウ： フィリップ・マーロウ，私立探偵です。
裁判長： 証人台に立って。　　　　　　　　　　　（足音）
検察官： マーロウさん，カート・ハーパーが殺害された7月30日の朝，あなたはこのハーパー氏によって私立探偵として仕事の依頼を受けましたか。

you hired as a private detective by the said Mr. Harper?

Mar: I was.

Pros: And at that time, Mr. Marlowe, did Mr. Harper state his reason for hiring you?

Mar: He did. He wanted me to act as his personal bodyguard on the following day when he planned to drive to San Francisco.

Pros: Did he say why he needed a personal bodyguard?

Mar: He did. He told me he was afraid for his life. He had refused a gambler's demand that he drug a certain race-horse a week earlier. And that gambler had threatened to kill him. (*hum of voices*)

Pros: I see. Now, Mr. Marlowe, did Mr. Harper name that gambler?

Mar: Yes, he did.

Pros: Who was it?

マーロウ： 受けました。
検察官： では，マーロウさん，その時ハーパー氏はあなたを雇った理由を述べましたか。

マーロウ： はい。氏は次の日に車でサンフランシスコへ行く予定で，その時の身辺警護に当ってほしいと言われました。

検察官： どうして護衛が必要なのか話してくれましたか。

マーロウ： はい。氏は自分の命が危ないと言われました。1週間前にある賭博師から，競馬の出場馬に薬物を与えてほしいと求められて断わったことがあり，その男に殺すと脅かされていたのです。（話し声）

検察官： なるほど。ではマーロウさん，ハーパー氏はその賭博師の名前を口にされましたか。
マーロウ： はい，言っておられました。
検察官： だれでした。

Mar:	**Earl Jurnigen.** (*hum of voices*)
Pros:	Thank you. No further questions, Your Honor.
Judge:	Counsel for the defense?
Defense:	The counsel for the defense waives cross-examination, Your Honor.
Judge:	(*gaveling*) **The witness is excused.**
Mar (Nar):	It didn't make sense, no cross-examination, because, from the opening adjective, the counsel for the defense — a dapper item named Calder who always appeared in French cuffs, grey gaberdine and a cocky, uninviting smile — had raved, ranted, and practically spit at each witness the state had presented. So the courtroom was left with the tingling impression that Earl Jurnigen's attorney had something of a surprise waiting up his legal sleeve. Later, when Calder was on his feet and addressing the jury, that something started out fast.
Defense:	**Now that the state has taken the trouble to offer so much circumstantial**

マーロウ：	アール・ジャーニギンです。（話し声）
検察官：	ありがとう。裁判長，質問は以上です。
裁判長：	被告側弁護人，発言がありますか。
弁護人：	弁護側は反対尋問を差し控えます。
裁判長：	（槌の音）証人は退席してよろしい。
マーロウ(語り)：	反対尋問がないというのは筋の通らないことだった。弁護人はコールダーという抜け目のない男で，袖口がフレンチ・カフスの，グレーのギャバジンの衣服に身を包み，気取って尊大な笑みを絶やさないやつだったが，この裁判のそもそもの始めから，検察側の繰り出す証人の1人ひとりに，どなり，あたりちらし，つばを吐きかけんばかりだったのだ。だから，法廷中の皆が，アール・ジャーニギンの弁護人は，何かあっというような手を用意しているらしいと思い，わくわくしていた。やがて，コールダーが立ち上がって陪審員たちに話しかける時になって，その手というのがすばやく繰り広げられることになった。
弁護人：	検察側は，状況証拠ばかりを，すなわち伝聞・うわさ・推測ばかりをわざわざお示しくださったが，弁護側としては，た

evidence, so much hearsay, rumor, conjecture — now I will smash all of that with the testimony of one man, one man known to all of you as an outstanding citizen of this city, a prominent real-estate broker, and an unimpeachable witness, eager to testify — Mr. Leonard Gaines.

Mar(Nar): It worked. Landed in each and every lap like a live grenade, and exploded all the way round at once. And when the eminent Mr. Gaines, grey at the temples, maybe 45, and neat in expensive midnight-blue flannel with giant stick, emerged and took the stand, and in his own meeting-of-the-board tone of voice told the court that Earl Jurnigen had spent the entire day and night of July 30th last with him at his Malibou Beach home, the prosecuting attorney's jaw dropped to his chest, and he stared dumb.

Gaines: No time during day or night did Mr. Jurnigen ever leave my home...and as for

ったお1人，皆さん方がご存知の当市の名士であり大不動産業者でもある方を，申し分のない証人とするだけといたしたい。証人は，証言に熱意をお持ちであり，それだけで検察側の証拠なるものはすべて一蹴されるでありましょう。レナード・ゲインズ氏にお願いいたします。

マーロウ(語り)： 　これは効いた。法廷の1人ひとりの膝元に手投げ弾がほうりこまれ，その全部が一度に爆発したようなものだった。高名なるゲインズ氏は，生えぎわに白髪の混じった45歳ほどの姿を高価な濃いブルーのフランネル・スーツにきちんと包み，大きなステッキをついて入廷すると，証人台に進み，重役会議向けの口調で，7月30日は昼夜ともマリブ・ビーチの自宅でアール・ジャーニギンと過ごしましたと証言した。これには検察官も口をあんぐりと開け，ものも言わずに目を見張るばかりであった。

ゲインズ： 　この日1日，昼も夜も，ジャーニギン氏は私の家から1歩も外へ出ておりません。さらに，殺人の時刻とされる8時に

the hour of the murder, 8:00 in the evening, we were having dinner. After that we played gin rummy until, oh... until midnight.

Defense: Are you sure of that, Mr. Gaines, the hour of your dinner, I mean?

Gaines: I am positive, Mr. Calder.

Gail: No, no, you can't be! You're lying!

Judge: Quiet, quiet! Order. Miss Harper, order in the court, please.

Gail: No, I won't be quiet. I won't any more!

Judge: Miss Harper! Quiet! Order! Order! (*sounds of gaveling*) This court is adjourned until tomorrow morning at ten o'clock.

(*music*)

は，私と2人で食事をとっておりました。その後，そう，真夜中まで，私どもはジン・ラミー（トランプ・ゲーム）をいたしました。

弁護人： ゲインズさん，確かでしょうね，その夕食の時刻は。

ゲインズ： 確実です。

ゲイル： 嘘だわ。そんなはずがないわ。でたらめよ。

裁判長： 静粛に。発言は許しません。ハーパーのお嬢さん，法廷ではお静かに。

ゲイル： いやよ。静かになんて。もう黙っているもんですか。

裁判長： ハーパーさん。お静かに。いけません。黙って。（槌の音）本法廷は明朝10時まで閉廷といたします。　　　（音楽）

2

Waitress: Another scotch and soda, mister?

Mar: Yeah, I guess so. Wait a minute, baby... I think I'm about to have company.

Gail: Mr. Marlowe, can I talk to you for a minute? I'm....

Mar: Gail Harper, yeah, I know. What I don't know is why you're not doing thirty days in the rock pile for that rumpus you just kicked up in court. Would you like a soft drink?

Gail: No, thanks.

Mar: Just one, baby.

Wait: Check.

Gail: The judge said he understood and let me off with a short lecture, which is what I'd counted on.

Mar: Ah...you mean all that fireworks in there was planned, and not just

(2)

ウェイトレス： ウイスキーソーダをもう1杯いかがですか。
マーロウ： そう，頼む。いや，待ってくれ。客がやって来そうだから。

ゲイル： マーロウさん，少しお話ししていいかしら。私……。

マーロウ： ゲイル・ハーパーさん。存じています。法廷であれだけ騒いだのに30日間のムショ送りにならなかったというのはなぜだかわかりませんがね。ソフト・ドリンクでもいかが。

ゲイル： 結構ですわ。
マーロウ： 1人分だけ頼む。
ウェイトレス： はい。
ゲイル： 裁判長は，気持ちはわかるといって，軽いお説教だけで許してくれたわ。計算通りよ。

マーロウ： ほう。じゃ，法廷の打ち上げ花火の一件は計画通りで，自然発火じゃなかったとおっしゃる。

spontaneous combustion?

Gail: That's right. I had to have time. Look, Mr. Marlowe, will you work for me?

Mar: Oh, now look...baby.

Gail: Will you help me prove that Mr. Leonard Gaines is a liar and that Earl Jurnigen did kill my father?

Mar: Take it easy, Gail, that's a big mouthful, you know.

Gail: Mr. Marlowe, listen, please! There isn't much time. We've got to prove this tonight or never. By noon tomorrow at the outside the case will go to the jury.

Mar: O.K. What do you want me to do?

Gail: Take over where I left off. But first, let's get out of here.

Mar: All right. Never mind that drink, miss. (*they begin walking*) Where do we start, honey?

Gail: With Leonard Gaines' ex-wife, Debbie Jansen....Here's a snapshot of her.

Mar: Mmm.

ゲイル： 　そうよ。時間をかせぎたかったの。ねえ，マーロウさん，私のために働いてくださる？
マーロウ： 　おっと，そんなこと言われたって，君。
ゲイル： 　私，レナード・ゲインズさんって人は嘘つきで，アール・ジャーニギンは父を殺した犯人だって証明したいのよ。助けてくださる？
マーロウ： 　まあまあ，ゲイルさん。そりゃ重大発言ですぞ。
ゲイル： 　マーロウさん，聞いて。お願い。あまり時間がないのよ。今夜のうちに証明しなくちゃ手遅れになるの。明日の昼になれば，法廷じゃこの件を陪審員にまかせてしまうわ。
マーロウ： 　わかった。私にどうしてほしいんです。
ゲイル： 　私が途中までやった仕事を続けてほしいの。でも，まずこの店から出ましょう。
マーロウ： 　いいだろう。君，さっきの注文は取り消しだ。（2人歩き出す）何から手をつけようか。
ゲイル： 　ゲインズの前の奥さんから。デビー・ジャンセンよ。これがスナップ写真。
マーロウ： 　ほほう。

Gail: They were divorced about six months ago, Mr. Marlowe, and she wasn't very happy about it.

Mar: No....Made you figure she was your in?

Gail: Yes, and I was right. Mr. Marlowe, it took eavesdropping, bribery, second-story work, but I found out plenty.

Mar: I'll bet you did. Like what?...Oh, hold, Gail; the light's red.

Gail: Like the fact that Debbie and a guy called Eugene Mallory are putting a bite on Gaines for twenty-thousand dollars. Blackmail, Mr. Marlowe, with the pay-off schedule to be made sometime tonight. Right now she's staying at the Sunland Sulphur Springs lodge out in the Valley. Gaines used to go there once in a while for his arthritis. And the point of the whole business is a letter Leonard Gaines once wrote to his ex-wife.

Mar: No fooling?

ゲイル：　　あの夫婦は半年ほど前に離婚したのよ，マーロウさん。でも，この女はそれが気にくわなかった。

マーロウ：　なるほど。で，その女を事件の突破口にしようと思いついた。
ゲイル：　　そう。思った通りだったわ。マーロウさん，私，盗み聞きをしたり，わいろをばらまいたり，夜盗のまねごとまでやったけど，ずいぶんいろいろとわかったことがあるのよ。
マーロウ：　そうらしいな。たとえばどんなこと？　お，ちょっと待った。信号が赤だ。
ゲイル：　　たとえばね，デビーとユージン・マロリーって男が，ゲインズから2万ドルまきあげようとしてたってこと。恐喝よ，マーロウさん。その支払いは今夜のうちに済ます予定らしいの。あの女，いまはバレーにあるサンランド硫黄鉱泉ロッジに滞在中よ。ゲインズは関節炎の治療に時たまこの温泉に行ってたの。で，恐喝のネタになっているのは，レナード・ゲインズが彼女にあてて書いた1通の手紙なのよ。

マーロウ：　本当かね。

Gail: Uh-huh.

Mar: (*laughs*) Tell me, what's that got to do with Jurnigen's trial and Gaines being a — oh, it's green now.

Gail: I think there's a connection, because yesterday I overheard Debbie tell this Mallory something about Gaines' scheduled appearance at the trial today....
(*loud horn and scream*)

Mar: Hey, hey. Those drunk California drivers!

Gail: The man behind the wheel....

Mar: What about him?

Gail: That thin face, blonde hair, I've seen him before. I know he was trying to hit one of us.

Mar: Oh, fine. Well, that will keep things from getting dull, won't it?

Gail: Then...then you're gonna help me?

Mar: Now look, I...(*laughs*), oh, who could resist you, baby? Okay, tonight I check in at the lodge at Sunland Sulphur Springs. Come on, let's get out of here.   (*music*)

ゲイル： 　そうよ。

マーロウ： 　（笑う）わからんね。何の関係があるのかね，ジャーニギンの裁判とゲインズの……お，青になった。

ゲイル： 　つながりがあると思うわ。今日の裁判でゲインズが出廷するって話は，昨日デビーがマロリーにしてたのよ。盗み聞きしたの。（鋭いクラクション。金切り声）

マーロウ： 　おい，コラッ。カリフォルニアには酔っぱらい運転が多くてね。
ゲイル： 　運転してたあの男……。
マーロウ： 　そいつがどうかしたかい。
ゲイル： 　細面で金髪，見覚えがある。私たちのどっちかをひき殺そうとしたんだわ。
マーロウ： 　結構。事件はますます面白くなりそうじゃないか。

ゲイル： 　じゃあ……やっぱり私を助けてくださるのね。
マーロウ： 　待ってくれ，それは……（笑う）やれやれ，君にはかなわんよ。承知した。今夜はサンランド硫黄鉱泉ロッジに泊まりに行ってみる。じゃ，行こうか。　　　　　　　　　　　　　　（音楽）

3

Mar (Nar): It was eight o'clock, and almost dark when I reached the foothills of the mountain range that separates the San Fernando Valley from L.A. proper. I turned off onto a narrow dirt road that ran through a twisting gorge, past a moonfaced watchman who asked no questions as he slowly opened a sagging wooden gate, faintly labelled 'Sunland Sulphur Springs,' where Mother Nature's remedies bubble from the earth private.

It was another five minutes along the same dirt road uphill, and through thick foliage, before I was at a parking space, out of my car and walking the last quarter of a mile toward the lodge itself, which was spotted with widely separated cottages, also, sagging, and each tagged 'Casa,' followed by something Spanish and hard to pronounce.

Inside the place was cheap porch furniture, and occasional threadbare rugs, of scarred pine; and it was deserted, except for a sleepy old guy, with thick-hooded eyes and an accordion-wrinkled face, who was slouched in a

(3)

マーロウ（語り）： 　おれが，ロサンゼルスの中心からサン・ファーナンド・バレーをへだてる山脈のふもとの丘陵に着いたころは８時，ほとんど暗くなっていた。狭い未舗装道路に入り，曲がりくねった谷の道を抜けて行くと，丸顔の番人が１人いた。こいつは質問をするでもなく，「サンランド硫黄鉱泉」とかすかに文字の残る傾いた門をゆっくりと開けてくれた。中には，母なる自然の妙薬である温泉が，施設の中に入った人だけのために，地中から沸き出しているのである。

　さらに５分，その未舗装道路を登って木々の濃い緑の中を進んでいくと駐車場に出た。おれは車を置いて，あとはロッジまで400メートルばかりを歩いた。あたりのあちらこちらに，これもパッとしないコテージが点在している。１軒１軒に，「何とか荘（カサ）」とスペイン語の読みにくい名前がつけてあった。

　事務所のポーチには安物の家具があり，ところどころにボロっちい足ふきが置いてある。床はきずだらけだ。眠たそうな年寄１人の他に人気はない。この老人，目の皮のたるんだしわくちゃ面で，カウンターの上の名札の陰にだらしなくつっぷしていた。名札にはれいれいしくも，夜間警備員メイナード・シャープ

heap behind a sign at the reservation desk that read 'Maynard Sharpe'no less, night manager. I gave him my name and said that both my rheumatism and I needed a rest. He came to, almost.

Sharpe: (*yawning*) Room, er, Mr. Marlowe? Well, let's see....I can let you have most any one of the cottages, half of them are empty.... Things come slow at this time of year.

Mar: How slow can you get?

Sharpe: You'd be surprised. How about 'Casa Francisco de Lions'?

Mar: 'Casa Francisco,'huh? Yeah, that'll be fine, Mr. Sharpe.

Sharpe: Alright, sir. Now, if you just sign the register here, I'll get your key....

Mar (Nar): As I signed my name I checked the guest list quickly, and the next second found what I wanted, Deborah Jansen, and next to that, in a different hand, her cottage for the night...'Casa

とある。おれは名を名のり，リューマチの治療に 1 泊したいのだと言った。ご老人はどうやらこうやら目を覚ましたようだ。

シャープ： （あくびする）部屋があるかですって？ えーと，マーロウさん。さて，と。……コテージのどれでも使ってください。半分は空なんですよ。今頃のシーズンは客足がのろくてね。

マーロウ： これ以上のろくなるのかね。
シャープ： あきれるくらいでさ。「フランシスコ・デ・リオン荘」はどうです。

マーロウ： 「フランシスコ荘」か。ああ，それでいいよ，シャープさん。

シャープ： じゃ，よろしいですね。この宿帳に署名していただいてからキーをお渡しします。

マーロウ(語り)： おれは署名しながらすばやく客のリストを調べ，すぐに，探していたデボラ・ジャンセンの名前を見つけた。その名の隣には違う筆跡で「ロランド・デ・バレンディド荘」と，泊まり先が記入してあった。まずまずの成果だ。まあここまでわ

Rolando de Barendido.' That's close enough. Well, anyway, that was all I needed. I took the key from Mr. Sharpe — a misnomer if ever you heard one — learned the location of my quarters, paid him in advance, and left.

Outside I turned to my right, past a large open bath that smelt like rotten eggs, and talked to itself like a junior Vesuvius, as more warm sulphur water, equally unpleasant to smell, bubbled from a pipe in the center. (*sound of water running*)

Beyond that was the first cottage, another 'Casa' I couldn't pronounce, and it stayed like that all the way down the line, until I reached the second one that showed light. It was the 'Casa' known as 'Rolando de Barendido,' and when I moved closer and around to a window with a screen only, I knew that my client had done her eavesdropping well. Becuse in the center of the room, putting on her coat was the ex-wife named Debbie. Standing nearby, and holding on tight to the cigarette in his hand like a support, was what had to be the boyfriend, Eugene Mallory.

かりゃいい。シャープじいさんからキーを受けとり——こんなもたもたした老人がシャープでは名前負けというものだ——，泊まるコテージの位置を教わってから，おれは前金で宿泊代を支払って事務所を出た。

　出たところで右に曲がった。腐った卵の匂いがする大きな野天風呂のそばを通っていく。硫黄混じりの湯が，これも不愉快な匂いを発しながら，中央のパイプからボコボコと流れ出し，ベスビアス火山の小型版よろしくの音を立てていた。（湯の流れる音）

　風呂の向こうにコテージが並んでいる。最初のコテージの何とか荘という字は発音できそうにもない。１列に並んだ他のコテージも同様だった。やがて，明かりのついているコテージをもう１軒見つけた。それが「ロランド・デ・バレンディド荘」だった。おれは近づいて，網戸を閉めてあるだけの窓のほうへまわってみた。これじゃゲイルも盗み聞きは楽だったろう。部屋の中央では，前夫人デビーがコートをはおりかけたところだった。その近くにつっ立って，手のタバコをしっかりと握って，それがなくちゃころんでしまうというような姿の男，こいつがボーイフレンドのユージン・マロリーに違いない。

Mallory: You're sure that Gaines will go thorough with this alright?

Debbie: For the hundredth time, Eugene, yes, I'm positive. Can't you understand he has to? Besides, twenty-thousand dollars won't break him — it won't more than bend him a bit. Now stop worrying.

Mal: But I can't. Debbie, why must you go alone? Why can't I go with you?

Deb: Eugene, please, we've been over that. I told Leonard that I'd meet him in town at the Beverly Crest Hotel at ten, and alone. He agreed to also be alone, except for the money.

Mal: Darling, you do handle things well. Come here, darling...and a kiss for your brilliant work....

Deb: Oh, please, Eugene. There isn't time.

Mal: What's the matter? Are my kisses losing their flavor at this point?

| マロリー： | ゲインズのやつ，この約束をちゃんと守ると思うのかい。 |

| デビー： | 百回も言ってるじゃない，ユージン。そうよ，大丈夫よ。あいつ，他に手はないのよ。それに，2万ドルばかり払ったって破産なんて男じゃないわ。ちょっとこたえるかなってくらいのところよ。心配するのはよしてちょうだい。 |

| マロリー： | 心配は心配だよ。デビー，どうして1人だけで出かけなくちゃいけないんだい。ぼくもついていくよ。 |
| デビー： | ユージン，ねえ，もう話し合ったことじゃない。市内のビバリー・クレスト・ホテルで10時に会う，1人で行くって，レナードに言ってあるの。あいつも1人で来ることに同意したのよ。ただし，金だけは持ってね。 |

| マロリー： | 君って何でも巧くできるんだな。ちょっとおいでよ。ごほうびにキスしてあげる。 |

| デビー： | いやねえ，ユージン。時間がないのよ。 |
| マロリー： | どうしたっていうんだ。ぼくのキスの味が落ちたとでもいうのかい。 |

Deb: Don't be a fool. Look, it's late, Eugene. It's after nine already. I've got to hurry. Now go on, go on. Be a good boy and leave now. We shouldn't even be seen together tonight.

Mal: Why not, Debbie?

Deb: It's not smart. Here. (*kisses him*) Meet me at the Tulip Room, darling, at eleven as we planned, and, Eugene, we'll have time and reason to relax...twenty-thousand bucks worth of reason. (*music*)

デビー： ばか言わないでよ。ほら，遅いのよ，ユージン。もう9時過ぎよ。急がなくちゃ。さあ，いい子だから帰ってちょうだい。今夜はいっしょのところを見られちゃ困るのよ。

マロリー： どうして困るんだい。

デビー： まずいんだったら。はい。(キスする) 計画通り，11時にチューリップ・ルームで落ち合いましょう。ねえ，ユージン，その時になったら，ゆっくりとくつろいで大丈夫なのよ。2万ドル分だけくつろいでいられるんだものね。　　　(音楽)

4

Mar(Nar): As Mallory oozed towards the door I slid away from the cottage, and into the shadow of a clump of trees nearby. I stayed there as he walkied outside down the road at the back of the parking space. Then a few minutes later, when Debbie clicked off the light and left, I moved out of hiding and started slowly after her at a safe distance, until from some place in the night an ugly, snub-nosed automatic that belonged to someone blonde and thin-faced, as at the near automobile accident, stopped me cold.

Langley: Where you goin', Jack?

Mar: For air. I love to walk in the country at night, O.K.?

Lang: I wouldn't know it, Jack. I'm a city boy myself, but as long as that's what you want, that's jake with me. As long as it's good and dark. Now, go on, that way, move! *(music)*

(4)

マーロウ(語り)： マロリーがドアの方へ動いたので，おれはコテージからそっと離れ，近くの木立ちの陰にすべり込んだ。マロリーが駐車場の向うの道路の方へ歩いていく間は隠れていて，数分後，デビーが明かりを消して出かけてから，こっちも木陰から出て，安全な距離を保ってゆっくりとあとを追っていった。しかし，闇の中から不恰好なずんぐり型のピストルがつきつけられ，おれは立ち往生した。ピストルを握っているのは，さっきの交通事故になりかけた時の，金髪の細面の男だった。

ラングリー： おっさん，どこへ行く？
マーロウ： 一息つきに行くんだ。おれは夜の田舎の散歩が好きでね。

ラングリー： わからんな。おれは都会育ちだから。でも，おっさんがそうしたいんなら構わんさ。うんと暗いところへ行ってもらおうか。さ，そっちだ。歩け，歩け。　　　　　　　　（音楽）

Lang: All right, Jack, that's far enough.... Hold it. Turn around and face me.

Mar: Why, so I can watch your pull the trigger?

Lang: Never mind why, just turn around.

Mar: O.K. Turn it is.

Lang: That's better. Now one step closer....

Mar: One step closer....

Lang: Hey, what's that? (*they fight*)

Mar: Not a present, my friend....Take 'em (*hits Langley*) Now, before I beat you to little pieces, we'll have it. Who are you? Who do you work for, and what do you want with me?   C'mon, come and talk!

Lang: O.K....O.K. No more. My name's Langley. I work for Earl Jurnigen. I've been watching you ever since the trial started. Jurnigen didn't want you moving in on him.

Mar: Which is why you tried to pick me off in a car when I was with Gail Harper this

ラングリー： よし，ここまで来りゃいい。止まれ。回れ右をしてこっちを見るんだ。

マーロウ： どうしてなんだ。ひき金を引くところをおれに見せてくれるっていうのか。

ラングリー： 理由なんかいい。こっちを向きなってんだ。

マーロウ： わかった，向くよ。

ラングリー： それでいい。いいか，一歩でも近づいたら……。

マーロウ： 一歩でも近づいたらどうするって。

ラングリー： おい，どうする気だ。（2人もみあう）

マーロウ： どうするったって大したことでもないがな，ほら。（ラングリーを殴りつける）さあ，バラバラにされないうちに話したらどうだ。名前は何だ。だれに雇われてるんだ。おれに何の用だ。さあ，言うんだ。

ラングリー： わ，わかった。もう殴らんでくれ。おれはラングリーってんだ。アール・ジャーニギンの仕事だよ。裁判の初めからあんたを見張ってた。ジャーニギンのだんなが，あんたに手を出されちゃ困るってんでさ。

マーロウ： そういうわけで，今日の午後，ゲイル・ハーパーとおれを車で轢き殺そうとしたんだな。そうだろう。

afternoon? Ha, come on!

Lang: Yeah, yeah, that's why. Now what are you going to do with me?

Mar: For the time being, buster, I'll leave you as it is...flat on your back, (*punches Langley*) because I've still got to catch up with a lady before she reads a letter....City boy!

ラングリー： そう，そうなんだ。で，おれをどうする気だ。

マーロウ： 今のところはな，そっとしておいてやる。おねんねしてもらってからな。（ラングリーを殴りつける）女が手紙の１文字だって読み上げないうちに追いつかなくちゃならんのだ。ふん，都会育ちの坊やめ。

5

Mar(Nar): It was strictly hit and run. I piled Langley into the manzanita and didn't even wait to see him bounce. Instead I took off toward a gully. There was a short-cut to my car, because I knew that Jurnigen's watchdog had nothing to offer, compared with a hot-headed Debbie Jansen, who at the moment no doubt was well on her way to the Beverly Crest Hotel. At the blackmail rendezvous it was a cinch to wind up at the final destruction of the letter. That was my theory, but I dropped it like a hot rock just as I crossed the path to the sulphur pool. (*scream*)

Sharpe: Mr. Marlowe, Mr. Marlowe, somebody screamed. There! In there by the screen. Oh, my gosh...oh, my gosh...

Mar(Nar): It was nothing but sulphur fumes and the gurgle of the stream, until Sharpe played his flashlight over the pool. Then, we saw her, in the

(5)

マーロウ(語り)： これぞまさに轢き逃げってやつだ。おれはラングリーをマンザニタのやぶの中へ投げこみ，はねかえるさまを見届けもせず，谷の方へと向かった。それが，おれの車を置いた場所への近道だった。ジャーニギンの番犬野郎などにはもう用はない。せっかちのデビー・ジャンセンが気にかかる。あの女はきっともうビバリー・クレスト・ホテルのずいぶん近くまで行っているだろう。恐喝の相手と出会えば，あの手紙が完全に処分されてしまうのは確実だ。この時のおれの推理はこんなところだったのだが，小道から硫黄風呂のそばへ出たとたんに，この考えはすっかり吹き飛んでしまった。　　　　　　　　　　　　　　　　　　(悲鳴)

シャープ： マーロウさん，マーロウさん，だれかの悲鳴だ。あそこだ！　その金網のわきだ。ああ，何てこった……ああ，どうしよう……

マーロウ(語り)： 初めのうちは，温泉の湯煙が見え，流れる水音が聞こえてくるばかりだった。が，シャープが懐中電灯を風呂に向けた時，女

water that was turning red from the blood oozing around the knife in her back.

Sharpe: Look, look! It's Miss Jansen.

Mar: Come on, Pop, give me a hand. Let's get her out of there. Come on, take it easy now, take it easy....That's it. Debbie!

Deb: I never should have tried it.

Mar: Tried what? Who was it, Debbie? Who did this?

Deb: He...got the letter....

Mar: Who? Who got the letter? Debbie, Debbie....

Sharpe: Marlowe....Did she...did she pass out?

Mar: For good, Maynard. She's dead.

Sharpe: Oh, well...she...she seemed to be mumbling something about a letter. Did you get what it was?

Mar: Only a part of it. The killer apparently took the letter away from her. Believe me, that's bad.

　　　　　　　の姿が見えた。女の背中に突き刺さったナイフの回りから血が流れ出して，温泉の湯を赤あかと染めていた。

シャープ：　　見てくれ！　あれはジャンセンさんだ。
マーロウ：　　じいさん，手を貸すんだ。女を中から引きあげるぞ。さあ，落ち着いて。あわてないで。そう，それでいい。デビーじゃないか。

デビー：　　やらなきゃよかった。
マーロウ：　　やらなきゃって何をだ。だれなんだ，デビー。こんなことをやったのは。

デビー：　　あいつ……手紙を取った。
マーロウ：　　だれのことだ。だれが手紙を取ったんだ。デビー，デビー。

シャープ：　　マーロウさん，その人，気を失ったのかね。
マーロウ：　　永久にな。死んでしまった。
シャープ：　　やれやれ。その人，何か手紙のことをもごもご言ってたようだったが，何の話かわかったかね。

マーロウ：　　一部だけだ。犯人はどうやらこの女の手紙を奪っていったらしい。まずいな，どうも。

Sharpe: Letter? Oh, what's a letter...?

Mar: Wait a minute, wait a minute....Oh, it's probably that pheasant again.

Sharpe: Letter? Pheasant? What are you talking about?

Mar: Oh, I guess I'm just getting jumpy.... Hey, hey. There is somebody. C'mon, Pop! (*footsteps*)

Sharpe: Sounds...sounds like he's over there, Marlowe.

Mar: Yeah, I can hear him. (*Marlowe shoots*)

Sharpe: Now that ain't going to do you any good, son; not in that bush, it ain't. What's more, I wouldn't go any further if I was you.

Mar: But, Pop, all the needs is ten seconds and he can destroy that letter for good.

Sharpe: Well, I'm just saying there's a million and one places a killer can hide in there and lay for you, Sonny.

Mar: Yeah, yeah, Pop. Well, at the moment

シャープ： 手紙ねえ。手紙なんかが一体何の――。

マーロウ： 待てよ，待ってくれ。なんだ，あの音はまた例のキジらしいな。

シャープ： 手紙だ，キジだって，あんたの言うことはわけがわからんよ。

マーロウ： いや，おれが落ち着かないってだけのことかな……いや，違った。だれかいるぞ。じいさん，来いよ。（足音）

シャープ： どうやら，あっちの方へ行ったらしいね，マーロウさん。

マーロウ： ああ，聞こえるよ。（ピストルを撃つ）

シャープ： あんた，撃ってみても仕方がなかろうぜ。こんな林の中だもの。それにさ，わしだったら，林の中へはこれ以上ふみ込んでは行かないね。

マーロウ： しかし，じいさん，10秒もあれば，あの手紙は破り棄てられて，なくなってしまうんだぜ。

シャープ： でもさ，ここらあたりにゃ，人殺しの隠れ場所になりそうなのがいくらだってあるからね，待ちぶせてるかもしらんよ。

マーロウ： そりゃそうだ。じゃ，今のところは身動きができないな。隠

it's a stalemate. I'd sure love to find out who that snake in the bush is.

Sharpe: You know, I've run a peaceful place up until it's getting to be like one of them there movies. The only thing left out is a posse.

Mar: Yeah, you're so right. Murders in the night,...lost letters....It's corny enough without a posse.

Sharpe: Yeah, and mighty dangerous, too.

Mar: Yeah, I see what you mean.

Sharpe: I'm ready to...to....

Mar: Yeah, I'm ready.

Sharpe: I'll lead you back to the office...I just don't understand this one bit. Miss Jansen is stabbed to death over that letter and....

Mar: Hey!

Sharpe: Huh....What is it?

Mar: Shhh...up ahead thre. Somebody got behind that big tree. Keep the chatter

れた悪党がどこのどいつか，ぜひ知りたいもんだ。

シャープ：　　いやはや，ここは，わしが見張ってて，何１つ事件なんか起きなかった場所なのにな。これじゃ活劇映画なみになってきたよ。これで警官隊でも出てくれば言うことなしだね。

マーロウ：　　そうだな，まったくだ。夜の殺人に行方不明の手紙。警官隊出動と来なくても，型通りもいいところだよ。

シャープ：　　そう，でも，なにしろぶっそうな話だ。
マーロウ：　　わかるよ。まったくそうだ。
シャープ：　　じゃあ，あの……そろそろ……。
マーロウ：　　ああ，そうだな。行くか。
シャープ：　　事務所まで道案内していくから。この事件はさっぱりわからんな。ジャンセンさんが手紙のことだか何だかで刺し殺されたなんて……。

マーロウ：　　おい。
シャープ：　　え，何かね。
マーロウ：　　しーっ。向こうの方だ。あの大きな木の陰にだれか隠れている。じいさん，おしゃべりを続けてくれよ。道を行ったり来たり

	going, man. Walk up and down the path. Don't let him know we've spotted him. Go on....Talk! Talk!
Sharpe:	Oh, OK. Sure, sure. As I say I didn't understand....
Mar (Nar):	As the old man grimly ad-libbed his way up the path I followed a few feet behind. When I got even with the tree, I turned suddenly and with three fast steps I grabbed him.
Mar:	Come here, you!
Sharpe:	Hang onto him.
Mar:	Well, Mr. Leonard Gaines, the unimpeachable citizen himself! Stand still, Gaines!
Gaines:	A gun! What's the idea, Marlowe?
Mar:	Try running and it'll come to you. I suppose you've got a legitimate reason for being here, all thought up.
Gaines:	I'm here because I...I've got a touch of

するんだ。おれたちに見つかったと悟られちゃまずい。さあ，おしゃべり，おしゃべり。

シャープ： ああ，わかったよ。やるよ。本当に訳がわからんがね。

マーロウ(語り)： 老人は道を歩きながら，思いつくままに何とか話をでっちあげていた。おれは1メートルばかり遅れてついていった。例の木と並んだところで，さっと向きを変えてすばやく3歩動き，その男を捕えた。

マーロウ： さあ，出てこい。
シャープ： 離すんじゃないぜ。
マーロウ： ほう，申し分のない名士，レナード・ゲインズ氏ご自身と来たね。動くなよ，ゲインズさん。

ゲインズ： ピストルを向けるのか。何のつもりだ，マーロウ。
マーロウ： 逃げたりしたらピストルがものを言うぞ。どうしてこんなところに来たか，理由はちゃんと考えてあるんだろうな。

ゲインズ： わしが来たのは……か，軽い関節炎を患っているから，治

	arthritis. I need a treatment and a night's rest.
Mar:	Arthritis isn't all you're going to have if I find what I think I'm going to find in your pockets. Empty 'em, buster...I said empty them.
Gaines:	Alright, I'll empty them.
Mar:	That's better.
Gaines:	Sharpe, you're witness; I demand that you....
Sharpe:	Now, just a minute, Mr. Gaines. You're in a pretty bad spot to demand anything.
Mar:	There, there's our baby...There's the letter we've been looking for. Pick it up, Gaines. Pick it up and read it.
Gaines:	Now see here, Marlowe....
Mar:	See there, Gaines. Read it while you're able to.
Gaines:	Yeah. "My dear Debbie, if I didn't know you so well, I'd resent your stupid accusations." Now, look, Marlowe....

療して一晩泊るつもりだったんだ。

マーロウ： あんたのポケットの中味がおれの予想通りだとしたら，関節炎だなんてのんきなことは言っておれなくなるぞ。ポケットの中味を見せてもらう。さあ，中味を出せ。出せと言ったんだ。

ゲインズ： わかった，出すよ。
マーロウ： それでいい。
ゲインズ： シャープ，証人になってもらうぞ，断わっておくが……。

シャープ： いや，ちょっと待った，ゲインズさん。あんた，断わっておくがなんて言える立場じゃありませんぜ。
マーロウ： ほら，それだ。それが探していた手紙だ。ゲインズさん，手に取って読んでもらおう。

ゲインズ： 無茶を言うな，マーロウ。
マーロウ： いいか，ゲインズ。読めといったら読め。

ゲインズ： わかったよ。「デビー様。ばかな非難をするものじゃない。君という人間がわかっていなければ怒るところだよ」もういいだろう，マーロウ。

Mar: Read it.

Gaines: "We've already made our property settlement, as you're well aware, and you'll be a long time finding a court that says otherwise. Now you know where you can go, so why not get started? As ever, Leonard."

Mar: Oh, fine. That's about as incriminating as a lecture on the family meat bill. Sharpe, whose jurisdiction are we under here?

Sharpe: Joshua —, why, er, the county sheriff's office.

Mar: Alright. Call him. Also call your men out on the highway and have them lock that main gate.

Sharpe: Main gate?

Mar: Yeah.

Sharpe: Say, now that's a good idea. I'll do it right now.

Mar: Wait a minute. Have you got a gun?

マーロウ: 止めるな。

ゲインズ: 「2人の財産の処分については，君も知っての通り，もう決まったことだ。どこの裁判所だって違った結論を出してはくれないだろう。君は，将来進みたい方向がはっきりしているのだから，ぐずぐずしていないで町を出た方がよい。敬具，レナード」

マーロウ: 結構な手紙だ。何もまずいところなんかない。家計簿の記入の仕方の指南書みたいなものだ。ところでシャープ，この辺はだれの管轄地域かね。

シャープ: ジョシュア何とかと言ったな，郡保安官の地区だよ。

マーロウ: よし，その人に電話したまえ。それから，表通りの方のお仲間とも連絡して，正門に鍵をかけてもらうんだ。

シャープ: 正門だって。
マーロウ: ああ。
シャープ: なるほど，そいつはいい考えだ。すぐ電話しよう。

マーロウ: ちょっと待った。じいさんは銃を持っているかね。

Sharpe: Yep, we've got a rifle, been in the family for years.

Mar: Can you use it?

Sharpe: Well, yeah, reckon I can. Where are you goin'?

Mar: Out to round up Langley. He'll be pushing hard to give his boss's star witness here a big helping hand. I want to be in shape to push back. And remember, Pop!

Sharpe: Yeah?

Mar: Keep your eye on Gaines, not on the phone, when you make those calls....I'll see you. (*music*)

6

Mar(Nar): For the second time that night I started down the hill toward the car lot, keeping in the shadows moving slowly this time, because it was odds on that Langley had taken everything

シャープ： 持ってるよ。昔からわが家に伝わったライフルなんだがね。

マーロウ： 使えるのかい。
シャープ： ああ，使えると思うよ。あんたはどこへ行くのかね。

マーロウ： ラングリーを見つけに行く。ゲインズは自分の親分の大事な証人なんだから，あいつめ，こいつを助けたがってちょっかいを出してくるだろう。はじきかえす備えをしておきたいんだ。それから，じいさん，もう1つ。

シャープ： 何かね。
マーロウ： 電話する時には，電話機じゃなくてゲインズだけ見てるんだぜ。じゃ，またな。　　　　　　　　　　　　　　　　（音楽）

(6)

マーロウ(語り)： おれは丘を下って駐車場へ向かった。今晩2度目だが，今度は物陰から出ないようにしてゆっくり下りていった。ラングリーのやつがきっと話を盗み聞きしていると思ったからだ。あいつは機会さえあれば，窮地におちいったゲインズを救うために，

in. And I knew he'd try to part my hair with a gun barrel to pull Leonard Gaines out of the jam he was in, the very first chance he had. So I stayed off the path long enough to have both socks full of burs when it happened...but not what I expected. (*gunshot*)

The Sharpe's family blunderbuss exploded with a blast like a small howitzer. So, also for the second time I turned and ran back up the hill this time to the office. I got there just as Maynard, climbing hand over hand up a smoking rifle barrel, made it to his feet.

Mar: Maynard! Maynard! What happened? Where's Gaines?

Sharpe: I don't know....Got away, I guess.

Mar: Well, the shot, what about that?

Sharpe: It went up there, through the roof.

Mar: Oh, fine.

Sharpe: Well, gosh, I...I didn't suspect a thing. He just said he wanted a smoke....

Mar: But he didn't happen to have a match,

おれの頭をピストルの銃身でぶちのめそうとするだろう。そういうわけで，道から離れたところを通っていったものだから，靴下には両方とも草の実がいっぱい付いた。その時……予想外のことが起こった。（銃声）

　シャープ家伝来のラッパ銃が小型曲射砲なみの爆発音をたてたのだ。そこで，おれはまたまた回れ右をして，今度は事務所の方へと坂を登っていった。着いてみると，メイナードは銃口から煙の出ているライフルの銃身に両手ですがりつきながら，ようやっと地面から体を起こしているところだった。

マーロウ： 　メイナード，メイナード。どうした。ゲインズはどこだ。

シャープ： 　わからん……逃げられたらしい。
マーロウ： 　撃った弾丸はどうなった。
シャープ： 　上へ行って屋根を突きぬけたよ。
マーロウ： 　すごいもんだ。
シャープ： 　その，実は，わし，まったくのんびり構えてたんだ。あいつが一服やりたいと言ったもんで……。
マーロウ： 　だけどマッチの持ち合わせがない，

I know. Oh, so you hung your rifle over your arms, stuck both hands in your pockets to find one for him, and that's when he took you.

Sharpe: Yeah, that's exactly what happened. How do you know?

Mar: Never mind, Pop.

Sharpe: I, I made a grab for him, though; ripped his coat about half way off.

Mar: Oh, that's great. That's great.

Sharpe: I'm sure sorry he got away.

Mar: Alright, don't worry about it, will you? He can't get far with the gate locked.

Sharpe: Well, I, er...I've got bad news there, too. Oh, the gate's locked all right, but there...there's a back road.

Mar: There's a back what?

Sharpe: A back road.

Mar: Road....Yeah?

Sharpe: It ain't much. It's rough and rocky, but it's passable. And...anybody who's been

って言ったんだろう，な。そこであんたはライフルを肩にかけて，両手をポケットに突っこんでマッチを探そうとした。そしたら，とたんにやつに襲われたんだな。

シャープ： ああ，まったくその通りだった。どうしてわかるのかね。

マーロウ： そんなことはいいよ，じいさん。
シャープ： でも，わしは逃げるやつをとっつかまえようとして，やつの上着をまっ二つに裂いてやったんだ。
マーロウ： そりゃ大したものだ。
シャープ： 逃がしちまって悪かったけど。
マーロウ： いいさ，気にしなさんな。正門が閉めてあるんだ，逃げきれやしないよ。
シャープ： その，そこもちょっとまずいんだ。いや，門は確かに閉めてもらった。だが，その……裏道があるんだよ。

マーロウ： 裏……何だって？
シャープ： 裏道だよ。
マーロウ： 道か。それで？
シャープ： 大した道じゃない。石ころだらけのでこぼこ道さ。でも，通っていけるんだ。ゲインズさんみたいにしょっちゅう来て

up here as often as Mr. Gaines has is sure to know about it.

Mar: Look, Pop. Can't you understand that there was a murder committed here tonight? We had the murderer....

Sharpe: But....

Mar: No buts. You fell for the oldest gag in the world. I was a sucker to turn him over to you. And will you stop waving that envelope?

Sharpe: I just think you ought to see this.

Mar: All right. What is it? Oh! Where did you get all that loot?

Sharpe: Gaines dropped it when I ripped his coat.

Mar: 'Twenty grand,' it says here on the wrapper. Something else is written here, too...'Casa Rolando de Barendido at ten'! Casa Ro...Pop, that's it! That's the answer. Come on! We've got to get down that back road, hurry! *(music)*

いる人なら，きっとその道を知っているはずだよ。

マーロウ：　　いいか，じいさん，今夜ここで起きたのは殺人事件なんだぜ。その人殺しのやつに，まんまと……。

シャープ：　　でも……。
マーロウ：　　でもってことがあるか。じいさんは古い古い手にひっかかったんだぜ。あの男をまかせたのはまずかったよ。頼むからそんな封筒をぱたぱたやるのをやめてくれないか。

シャープ：　　だって，あんたが見たいんじゃないかと思ってさ。
マーロウ：　　わかったよ。何かね。ほう。そんな大金，どこで見つけたんだい。

シャープ：　　ゲインズの上着を裂いてやった時に，落っことしていったんだ。
マーロウ：　　包みの上に「2万ドル」と書いてある。こっちにも文字がある……。「ロランド・デ・バレンデイド荘にて10時」ロランド荘か。じいさん，わかったぞ。これで読めた。行こう。その裏道を下りていくんだ，急げ。　　　　　　　　　　（音楽）

7

Mar (Nar): With Sharpe at the wheel of the pick-up truck, we bounced over the parallel, sometimes parallel, ruts, studded with stones the size of bowling balls. It was called a back road. It was the better part of two miles before he cut lights and whispered that if Gaines was not yet got stuck at all, it was sure to happen in a dry wash just around the next bend. I told him to wait, and went ahead on foot. He was right. Gaines was stuck in more ways than one. His car was up to its hubcaps in sand, and he was walled up to his hand compartment in blackmail, conducted by his ex-wife's murderer with the same letter she'd had. The letter. Eugene Mallory, in his clenched hand, had a tattered white envelope, nothing more. I held my '38 in close to my side, and edged up behind them.

Mal: ...about twenty-thousand....

Gaines: Mallory, I don't have that much.

(7)

マーロウ(語り)：　小型トラックをシャープじいさんに運転してもらって，おれたちはボーリングのボールなみの石がごろごろころがり，車のわだちの跡もめちゃめちゃに乱れている道を急いだ。それが裏道だった。たっぷり3,000メートルの余も行ったところで，シャープは車の明かりを消し，小声で言った。ゲインズの車がこれまで無事だとしても，次の角を曲がったところ，川の干上がっているあたりで，動きがとれなくなるはずだ，と。おれはじいさんに待っていろと言って，先へ歩いた。じいさんの言う通りだった。ゲインズは二重の意味で動きがとれなくなっていた。やつの車はホイールキャップまで砂にうずまってしまっていたし，やつ自身は，恐喝に会って雪隠づめの目にあわされていた。前夫人の殺人犯人が，女の持っていた手紙を種にゆすっていたのだ。手紙とはいっても，ユージン・マロリーが握りしめていたのは，しわくちゃの白い封筒だけだった。おれは38口径のピストルを横に構えて，2人の後ろにまわっていった。

マロリー：　2万ドルのことだが……。
ゲインズ：　マロリー，わしはそんな大金は持っていない。

Mal: You liar! You were going to pay her that.

Gaines: I don't know.

Mal: I know because we...we worked the deal out together, only she got greedy.... Tried to double-cross me and pull it off alone.

Gaines: Oh. So you killed her?

Mal: Yes. I didn't intend to, but when I found out that she'd tricked me I, I...was furious. The first thing I knew was that I'd stabbed her. That's enough of that. Just give me the money. You've nothing to worry about.

Gaines: Now, listen, Mallory....

Mal: No, you listen, Gaines. You're in no position to bargain. It's better than having your two hundred thousand dollar gambling debt exposed, your reputation ruined, isn't it? Or facing the triggerman, Langley, if you refuse to alibi for

マロリー：　　　　嘘つきめ。あの女にそれだけ払う予定だったじゃないか。

ゲインズ：　　　　何のことだ。

マロリー：　　　　わかってんだぞ。おれたちは2人で組んでやってたんだからな。ところが，あの女，欲を出しやがった。おれを裏切って1人で全部せしめようとしやがったんだ。

ゲインズ：　　　　そうか，それで殺したというのか。

マロリー：　　　　そうさ。やる気はなかったんだが，だまされたとわかってカッとなってな。気がついたら，あいつを刺してたんだ。そんな話はもういい。金を出せって言ってるんだ。お前は心配しなくたっていい。

ゲインズ：　　　　ちょっと聞いてくれ。マロリー。

マロリー：　　　　おまえこそ聞け。取り引きなんぞできる立場かよ。賭博で20万の借金があるとばれて，信用を落とすよりましじゃないか。それとも，ジャーニギンのアリバイ証言を断わって，殺し屋のラングリーに狙われる方がいいのか。いや，アリバイ証言をやってのけて，偽証罪に問われたいのか。見ろ，おまえは八方ふさがりなんだぞ。金を払うんだな。たったの

	Jurnigen, isn't it? Or bucking a perjury charge if you do alibi? Oh, no....You've got yourself in a corner again. Pay off! It's only twenty grand.
Gaines:	But I tell you, Mallory, I don't have it.
Mal:	You're lying.
Mar:	No, he isn't it! Don't move, either one of you. Leave your hands where they are. I've got twenty grand right here, and it's pretty well earmarked as blackmail payment already. Just to round things out, Mallory, I'll take that envelope you've got there.
Mal:	This? What do you want this for?
Mar:	Funny man....Because it's no doubt postmarked with an hour, a date and a location, which together with Brother Gaines' own handwriting places him out of town on July 30th — a time he swears he was at his Malibou home all day with Jurnigen. Right, Gaines?

2万ドルじゃないか。

ゲインズ： でも，マロリー，本当にその金が手元にないんだ。
マロリー： 嘘をつけ。
マーロウ： いや，嘘じゃないんだ。2人とも動くなよ。両手はそのままにしていろ。2万ドルはこの通りおれが持っている。こいつが恐喝の支払い金だってことは明明白白だ。もう1つ，念のために，マロリー，おまえの持ってる封筒をもらっておくとしよう。

マロリー： これか。こんなもの，何で必要なんだ。
マーロウ： 笑わせるな。その封筒には，時間と日付と場所を示す消印が押してあるはずだ。ゲインズ旦那の自筆の文字も入っているから，7月30日には，ゲインズはロサンゼルスにいなかったことがわかるはずだ。一日中，ジャーニギンとマリブの家にいたって誓ってたけどな。そうだろう，ゲインズ。

Gaines: Smart boy, aren't you, Marlowe?

Mal: You've still got a chance, Gaines. You better gamble with me. You've got nothing to lose now.

Gaines: I'm with you.

Mar: Stand still, buster! Or so help me, I'll....

Mal: Now Gaines....Go! (*gunshot*)

Gaines: Ohh...oh, my leg....

Mar: Were you thinking of going someplace, Mr. Gaines?

Gaines: No....No, I...I'm not going anyplace. Mr. Marlowe. (*music*)

ゲインズ：	なかなか頭が切れるな，マーロウ。
マロリー：	ゲインズ，まだチャンスはある。おれの方に賭けてみないか。こうなったら，それも損にはならんぞ。
ゲインズ：	承知した。
マーロウ：	動くんじゃない。動いたりすると，一発おみまいするぞ。
マロリー：	ゲインズ，さあ，逃げるんだ。（銃声）
ゲインズ：	ああっ……足が……
マーロウ：	ゲインズさんよ，どこかへお出かけかね。
ゲインズ：	いや，いや，マーロウさん，どこへも行きません。（音楽）

8

(*back in courtroom*)

Mar: Well, Gail, the big show's about to start. The court will be in session in a few minutes.

Gail: I know, and different from yesterday. Oh, you did a swell job, Mr. Marlowe. Gee, gee, I don't know how to thank you.

Mar: Save it, baby. If that scale Lady Justice holds in her hands is in better balance today, it was your hunch and old Maynard's blunderbuss did as much to put it there as my running around through the brush of Sulphur Springs!

Gail: But all I knew was that Gaines was lying. I didn't know it was as complicated as it was.

Mar: That's because Debbie Jansen was twice as treacherous as we figured.

⑻

（ふたたび法廷）

マーロウ： さあ，ゲイル，大した見物が始まるぜ。あと数分で開廷だ。

ゲイル： そうね，昨日とは大違い。本当に，マーロウさん，すばらしいお仕事ぶりだったわ。お礼の言葉もないくらい。

マーロウ： お礼なんかいいさ。正義の女神の天秤（てんびん）が今日は正確だとしたら，おれが硫黄鉱泉の林を走りまわったためもあるけど，君の直感とメイナードじいさんのラッパ銃のおかげなんだから。

ゲイル： でも，私にわかってたのは，ゲインズの言葉が嘘だってことだけよ。こんなにこんがらかった事件なんて思いもよらなかったわ。

マーロウ： そりゃ，デビー・ジャンセンが予測も出来ない裏切りをやってたからだよ。

Gail: I still don't understand. How did you know that Eugene Mallory had killed Debbie?

Mar: Oh, you'll see, baby. I overheard her tell Mallory that she was going to meet Gaines in the Beverly Crest Hotel at ten o'lock, for the pay-off. but I figured that was a lie, strictly for Mallory's benefit when Pop gave me the packet of money Gaines had dropped. It had that complicated name of a cabin and the time of the appointment, which was also 'ten' written on it. So I knew the real meeting was scheduled to take place out there. See?

Gail: Oh, I see. Then she was going to send Mallory off to the Beverly Crest, while she collected the money at Sulphur Springs and then beat it alone.

Mar: That's it, honey. You see, if her cabin had been named something simple like,

ゲイル： まだはっきりしないんだけど，ユージン・マロリーがデビーを殺したってことがどうしてピンときたの。

マーロウ： それはこうなんだ。デビーが金の受け取りにビバリー・クレスト・ホテルで10時にゲインズと会う予定でいるってことは，デビー自身がマロリーに説明したのを聞いていた。ところが，ゲインズの落としていった金包みをじいさんに見せられて，その説明はマロリーに聞かせるだけの嘘っぱちなんだとわかったのさ。金包みには，コテージの厄介な名前と，会う予定の10時という時間も書きつけてあった。そこで，本当の会合地点はあの温泉地の中なんだと見当がついたのさ。わかったかい。

ゲイル： わかったわ。じゃ，あの女は，マロリーがビバリー・クレスト・ホテルへ行くようにしむけておいて，自分じゃ温泉の中で金を受け取って1人でドロン，というつもりだったのね。

マーロウ： そうなのさ。あのコテージが，たとえば4号館というような単純な名前になっていたら，ゲインズにも覚えられたんだろう

er, Number 4, then Gaines could have remembered it. Instead of that, 'Casa Robino del Bangadolo,' (*they laugh*) or whatever it was, he had to write down, you see. Well...things might have been different.

Gail: Ah...you'd have found a way. After all you figured it was the postmark that was important.

Mar: Only after I'd been slapped in the face by a perfectly harmless letter with no envelope. It had to be the postmark. What else?

(*court official's voice*)

Gail: Oh, they're starting.

Mar: Yeah.

Gail: Good luck, Mr. Marlowe. Give 'em the works.

Mar: Don't worry, baby....I'm the eager witness today. We're going to knock them dead, literally. Ha! Ha! They've got

が，「ロビノ・デル・バンガドロ荘」とか何とか（2人笑う）と来たもんだから，書きとめておくしかなかったのさ。頭に入れておける名前だったなら，事態は変ってただろうな。

ゲイル： でも，あなたのことだもの，何とか謎を解いたでしょうよ。消印に意味があることだって，あなたの推理でわかったんだもの。

マーロウ： そいつは，封筒ぬきの手紙がまったくどうという中味のないものだったってことで，やっとハッと気がついて，それからあとの話さ。そうなってくりゃ消印にしか意味がないことになるからな。

（裁判所の係官の声）

ゲイル： 裁判が始まったわ。

マーロウ： そうだな。

ゲイル： しっかりね，マーロウさん。やっつけてやってよ。

マーロウ： まかせてくれ。今日はおれが熱意ある証人さ。悪党どもを完璧に打ちのめして死刑に追いこんでやる。ハハハ，天罰さ。

Mar (Nar): I watched Jurnigen's face as the preliminaries got under way. The killer was beaten. The court finally settled down to work and the prosecutor took over. I listened to his deft build-up, as he primed the jury, and the dramatic ringmaster voice he used when he called....

Pros: Will Philip Marlowe take the stand, please? (*music*) Now, Mr. Marlowe, you told us yesterday that you are a private investigator. Now will you tell the court in your own words what happened to you last night?

Mar (Nar): I sat there looking into the cold, baleful eyes of the prosecutor, and thought of a paraphrase on that wonderful quote from Oliver Wendell Holmes. 'It's not enough to ask for justice. One must also hope for mercy.'

マーロウ(語り):	裁判の準備段階が進められていく間，おれはジャーニギンの顔を眺めていた。この人殺しも，今日は打ちのめされていた。裁判がようやく本格的に動き出し，検察側の出番になった。検察官は陪審員への説明に，事件を手ぎわよく要約してみせてから，サーカスの団長よろしくの芝居がかった口調で言った——。
検察官:	フィリップ・マーロウさん，証人台にお立ちください。（音楽）さて，マーロウさん，あなたが私立探偵であることは昨日うかがいました。そこで，昨夜どういうことがあったか，ご自身の口から法廷の皆さんに話していただけますか。
マーロウ(語り):	おれは座って，検察官の冷たくおそろしい目を見つめ，オリバー・ウェンデル・ホームズのあの名文句を少し違った形で思い起こしていた——。「正義を求めることだけでは十分ではない。人は慈悲をも望むべきなのだ」

Pros: Mr. Marlowe....

Mar: Mmm? Oh...oh, yes, I'm sorry. Well, it began here in this room yesterday afternoon at about 3:30, when the counsel for defense called a witness, Mr. Leonard Gaines, to the stand.... (*music*)

THE END

検察官： マーロウさん。

マーロウ： え？ あ，ああ，失礼しました。さて，話は，昨日午後3時半，この部屋ではじまりました。あの時，被告弁護側は，レナード・ゲインズ氏を証人台に呼ばれたのでしたが……。

(音楽)

終

〈イングリッシュトレジャリー・シリーズ⑰〉
マーロウ証言に立つ

2006年8月25日　初版発行Ⓒ　　　　（定価はカバーに表示）

訳　者　青木信義
発行人　井村　敦
発行所　㈱語学春秋社
　　　　東京都千代田区三崎町2-9-10
　　　　電話 (03)3263-2894　振替 00100-7-122229
　　　　FAX (03)3234-0668
　　　　http://www.gogakushunjusha.co.jp
　　　　こちらのホームページで，小社の出版物ほかのご案内をいたしております。

印刷所　文唱堂印刷

落丁・乱丁本はお取替えいたします。